My Super Self Esteem

Written by Dania C. Binns

Illustrated by Alisha

ISBN: eBook
978-976-97229-6-5

ISBN: Paperback
978-976-97229-5-8

ISBN: (Hardcover)
978-976-97229-4-1

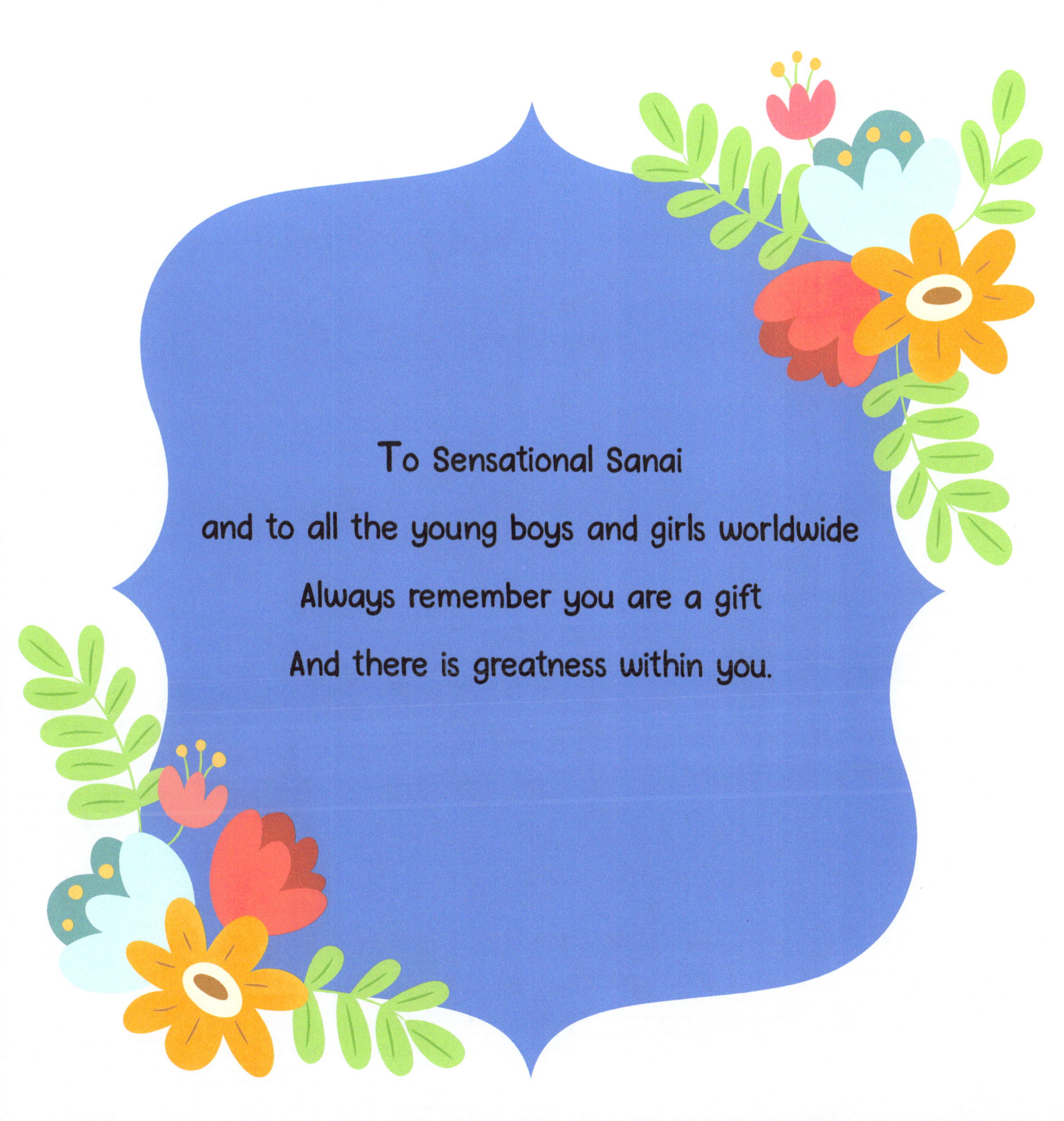

To Sensational Sanai
and to all the young boys and girls worldwide
Always remember you are a gift
And there is greatness within you.

I am Amazing
I am Adventurous
I know my Grandma is always generous
01

I am Bold
I am Beautiful
I love my Daddy and I think he's wonderful

I am Curious
I am Cute
I love my Mommy and she loves me too
03

I am Delightful
I am Daring
I have a Grandpa who is cool and caring
04

I am Energetic

I am Expressive

I know I will always be impressive

I am Fabulous
I am Friendly
I have a friend who is always trendy

I am Grateful
I am Gifted
And I am never going to get that twisted

I am Happy
I am Healthy
I will grow up to be wise and wealthy
08

I am Intelligent
I am Invincible
I will live my life on basic principles

I am Jovial

I am Just

I love my vegetables, yes, it's a MUST!

I am Kind
I am Keen
I know it's weird, but I love to eat green beans
11

I am Lovely
I am Light
I know I always think that I am right
12

I am Magnificent

I am Mighty

I got my score sheet and my average is ninety

I am Nurtured
I am Neat
I spread my bed with blankets and sheet

14

I am Original
I am Observant
I think my big brother believes I am his servant
15

I am Patient
I am Peaceful
I love my dog as he makes me cheerful

I am Qualified
I am Quick
I have an Uncle who always plays his tricks
17

I am Royal
I am Radiant
I love colors that are vibrant

I am Skillful
I am Strong
I live with purpose and will not be wrong
19

I am Thoughtful

I am Thankful

I have a teacher who says I am a handful

I am Unique
I am Unstoppable
Nothing that I want to be is impossible
THIS CITY NEEDS A HERO
21

I am Vibrant

I am Valuable

My Grandparents says I am adorable

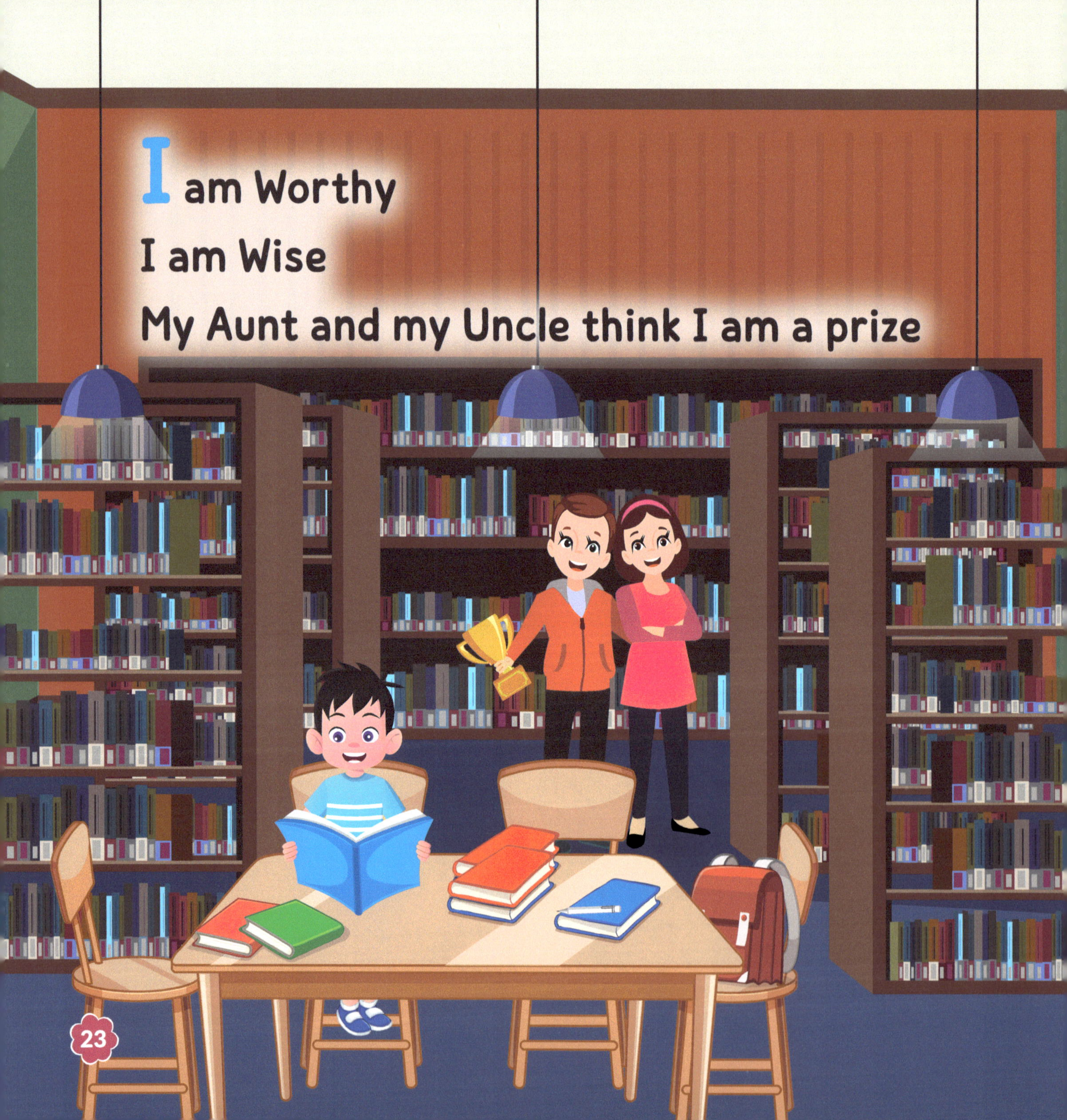
I am Worthy
I am Wise
My Aunt and my Uncle think I am a prize
23

I am Xenial (warm or welcoming)

I am eXciting

I have a journal that I always write in

I am Youthful
I am Yielding
I have a book that I am always reading

25

I am Zesty

I have Zeal

Look out world! For my big REVEAL!